Poems

A Place Where Secret Shadows Shine

Alice Smith

Copyright © 2014 by Alice Smith
First Edition – June 2014

ISBN
978-1-4602-4246-9 (Hardcover)
978-1-4602-4247-6 (Paperback)
978-1-4602-4248-3 (eBook)

All rights reserved.

No part of this publication may be reproduced in any form, or by any means, electronic or mechanical, including photocopying, recording, or any information browsing, storage, or retrieval system, without permission in writing from the publisher.

Produced by:

FriesenPress
Suite 300 – 852 Fort Street
Victoria, BC, Canada V8W 1H8

www.friesenpress.com

Distributed to the trade by The Ingram Book Company

Here is what people are saying about Alice Smith's poetry.

"Alice Smith's poems are like the roof crashing in or the ground swelling up. You're surrounded by ordinary things - a marriage, a mother and her dog, a sanitized front lawn, the bedside clock at midnight - when suddenly, things explode. In one line or a handful of words, Smith is able to transform the everyday into the sacred and the beautiful. That is the gift of poetry, and Smith reminds us to pay sweet attention to the small things before us. That's where the meaning is."

David Cook - columnist for the
Chattanooga Times Free Press

Inviting Truth to shine your rays of realness on the secrets stowed below, Alice Smith lures us across the threshold of her secret inner world, a world which we quickly recognize as our own. Whether walking in the woods, down a wedding aisle, or following the fading footprints of a night-time dream, her poetic offerings bring our own secrets to consciousness where they can be embraced and honored. Good poems serve this essential mysterious purpose, and these soul-full selections meet the test.

Jerry R. Wright - Jungian Analyst

Alice Smith's voice is one to be heard. Her words evoke feelings of wisdom and truth, of delight and regret, as she writes about coming full circle in life. She writes about the familiar insecurity we all know in childhood, and relives that in "Brown" as she dresses for a date after divorce. She writes of coming of age, and compares her two marriages, showing disappointment without a trace of bitterness. She marvels

A Place Where Secret Shadows Shine

over the good in life. Her words bring the reader to despair, then describe hope and the beautiful shining moments of life so clearly it is palpable. She writes, "Nothing is ever perfect, yet everything's complete."

> Ferris Kelly Robinson, author of Dogs and Love - Stories of Fidelity, and Never Trust a Hungry Cook

These poems are about this very moment, and yet they also (and sometimes at the same time) go way back, way forward, and way deep--with beautiful, fresh metaphor and surprise at all the right places. Once you start you are pulled through to the end. What a pleasure to read and learn about yourself—taught by the poems, the art, of a poet who is exploring everything within reach, and learning about herself.

> Clyde Edgerton, author of Walking Across Egypt and The Night Train

Alice Smith's collection of spare, beautiful poems actually functions as a memoir, the faithful record of a conscious life. Family forms the constant yet ever-changing circle of her world, as love brings joy, then pain, then joy again. From child to girl to wife and mother, a woman's entire journey is mapped in these pages, and an enviable wisdom is born. As all good poetry does, A PLACE WHERE SECRET SHADOWS SHINE has made me look at my own life in a more attentive and appreciative way.

> Lee Smith, author
> Hillsborough, N.C.

Sacred Idleness	*1*
Memory	*2*
Fall	*3*
Curious	*4*
Gramma's Grand	*5*
What's Most Important	*7*
Subtraction and Addition	*8*
Closing In	*9*
Rock a bye Baby	*10*
Living Color	*11*
Time Passes	*12*
Turn Around	*13*
Talking to Truth	*14*
Now That I Am Older	*15*
Moving On	*16*
When Pain Comes Knocking	*17*
My Beautiful Sister	*18*
My Best Friend	*19*
Killing the Tooth Fairy	*20*
Falling Apart	*21*
Binding Friendship	*22*
My Only Brother	*23*
Peace	*24*
Dream Mending	*25*
Crawling into the Future	*26*
Brown	*27*
Moving Through the Walls	*28*
Breathing in the Dawn	*29*
Winter Light	*30*
Liz	*31*
Donna Juan and I	*32*
Living On	*33*
Seeing the Ordinary	*34*
Where Would You Rather Be?	*35*
My Father	*36*
The Upper Lake	*37*

Reflections	*38*
Two Lovers	*39*
Simply Being There	*40*
Curly Hair	*42*
Dreams Can Change	*43*
Wedding Picture	*44*
Somewhere Over the Rainbow	*45*
Bumping and Twirling	*46*
Her in Me	*47*
Nelson's Pitcher	*48*
Evolving	*49*
Dream Work	*50*
Knotted Nots	*51*
Something Missing	*52*
Acceptance	*54*
Making a Mark	*55*
Something New	*56*
Buried Anger Takes Flight	*57*
Wow, I Carried On!	*59*
Out of our Control	*60*
Kenyan Kindness	*61*
Filling the Home	*62*
Dreaming Differently	*63*
Living in the Loop	*64*
Saving Thyme	*65*
Time after Time	*66*
Such a Kind	*67*
My Lonely Shoes	*68*
Floating in the Balance	*69*
What Is	*70*
The Garden and the Lake	*71*

This book of poetry is dedicated to my husband Alfred. He accepts me as I am and praises what I write. I have accused him many times of having low standards in wine, women, and song. Perhaps this list should include poetry. No matter what his standards are, his love and support mean the world to me.

I would also like to recognize my dream group. These wonderful women have helped me delve into dream life as well as waking life, in a way I never imagined possible.

Sacred Idleness

The soul hungers for a taste
of nothing.
Slip into the chasm of stillness
and breathe
melodious silence.
The hallowed hollow of splendid peace
holds the hush
of the half-note rest.
Mysterious intermissions are woven together
in an intricate pattern of
void.
Touch the tapestry of empty space
hanging
in the pale
quiet
sacred idleness.

Memory

Memory has a curious kin
to truth; a relative but not a twin.

The garden of roses,
A patch of mint,
The feather pillow with Mama's scent.

Fragments written in permanent ink,
blotches and blots indelibly linked.

A lover's touch,
A father's tone,
Disease that strikes a brother's bone.

This word italicized, that page erased,
One moment gone, another faced.

A broken marriage,
An unknown plight,
New love's sudden splash of light.

The years that pass as a blurry hint,
Or a block of time in boldest print,
Every word is written within.
It's all a part of what I've been.

Alice Smith

Fall

Afraid she might be noticed,
    she hid her frizzy fear
    in the corner cardboard kitchen
    playing all alone
    that kindergarten year.
The pageant produced a panic
    when she was chosen out of all
    to parade behind the king and queen
    and play the part of fall.
Winter, spring, and summer
    wore sparkly sequined tutus.
Winter twinkled in snowy white.
Spring and summer glittered
    in different shades of green,
    but nothing shined on fall.
Some seamstress mother
    created the humiliation
    the other season wore.
The homemade layers
    of multi-colored netting
    lay limp and lifeless.
Like autumn leaves,
    she wanted to be raked away.
Her fear was confirmed,
    The Ugliest of All
    as she trailed behind the king and queen
    the night they made her fall.

Curious

A giant butterfly
covers the sweater
that warms
the tiny toddler
standing in a yard
of multi-colored leaves.
Her smiling gaze
has spotted something
down below.
I wonder what
she sees.

Alice Smith

Gramma's Grand

When I was four years old
Gramma's grand piano
seemed dwarfed by the grandeur
of her royal living room
laden with marble table tops
and mirrors with golden frames.
In my early years
I had a talent creating sound
that was music to my ears.
I would finish my concerto.
and Gramma laughed and cheered.
When I was five
something odd had happened.
Somehow I had lost
what I had known before.
I banged and clanged and made some noise
that didn't sound like music.
I was royally confused
when Gramma laughed and cheered.
It took years for me to understand
It wasn't something I had lost
but something I never had.
The piano and the stately room
no longer seemed as grand
as other places in her home
like the kitchen with custard boiling
or the den where the pugs were allowed to play.
Outside Gramma's living room
were rockers and a glider
on a screened-in sitting porch
that overlooked the lilies of the valley.
I glided while she rocked
and sang a song about a man
who washed his face in a frying pan
and died with a toothache in his heel.
I always asked about her friend
who had the funny Fanny name,
Edith Ada Anna Bell Narcissus Fanny Yell.
She tickled my funny bone
in her warm, old fashioned way.

When I was 29 my grandmother passed away,
but unlike my piano playing
she isn't something I have lost.
She's something I'll always have.
Writing these words I still can hear
how Gramma laughed and cheered.

Alice Smith

What's Most Important

I was fourteen
when he called to ask me out.
He was older and wiser
like someone seventeen.
Three years was like three decades,
or so it seemed to me.
He wore the pants.
I cooked the meals,
just as things should be.
The marriage rolled along,
and then it bumped about
until the wheels fell off.

We called for help.
The helper asked,
"What's most important in your life?"
His answer had to do with health in Alabama.
Shit, I thought.
My answer tasted wrong
way before I spit it out.
He always had the right response
while mine seemed somehow lacking.
He cared for strangers
living in another state.
His vision carried weight.
Why was mine so close to home
clutched in a personal tote?
The marriage helper turned to me.
I shrugged and bowed my head.
"Our family,"
was all I said.

I'm proud to say
my answer is the same today.
I have a different outlook,
and I have a different husband.
Now I'm the one who's older,
older by a month.
A month is like a minute,
or so it seems to me.

Subtraction and Addition

One crosses
the threshold
and sucks
the oxygen
from the room.
The other's presence
adds oxygen
to the place
by giving those around him
plenty
of breathing space.

Alice Smith

Closing In

A narrow little figure
wearing worn-out gray-flannel fear
sits uncomfortably in a dim corner.

Across the room a naked nook
holds a larger restless form
wrapped in a comforter of complaint.

Locked in place by deadbolt security,
the immobile pair confine themselves
to the overheated space, cold and divided.

At night she draws the drapes and he puts out the light.
Dawn brings another day of lifeless life
making fear of death no longer such a fright.

Rock a bye Baby

Watch out baby!
The cradle will fall.
There is no grounding
rocking in the tree tops
bound in a bassinet.
The bough will break,
and your crib will crash
landing where you need to be.
Get up on your knees.
Crawl out of your crib.
See what lies below.
Finger the grass
then dig in the dirt
discovering what lives beneath.
When you have grown enough
to stand up on your feet
grab a limber limb,
climb through
the sturdy branches,
and look at the cradle
lying down below.

Alice Smith

Living Color

Images emerge from yesteryear
   as I wander back to before.
An innocent girl changing her look
   with colors she found in a drawer.
She pulled out the costume makeup box
   and put on a fancy face,
Rosed her lips and plummed her cheeks
   inventing a grownup place.
She hiked up her gown of flannel pink
   and pinned it nice and tight,
      wobbling around in plastic high heels
         giggling at the sight.

That world was black and white
   when *Father Knows Best*
   lived in the talking box.
When innocence dies the soothing rhyme is lost,
   and vivid shades of life bleed through.
This troubled time is shot in living color.
   Piercing sound bites,
     shattered images,
       disturbing tones
         clash in my imagination
         and leave me longing
           to live in black and white.

Where is the key to the costume box
   and the magic makeup drawer
      holding the hues of hope
         that colored life before?
The key is in experienced hands.
There's hope in eyes that see
the past with a sense of humor
   and set the magic free.
Tonight I'll wear a fuchsia gown
and crimson-red high heels.
I'll rose my lips and plum my cheeks
and dance into the colorful grayness.

A Place Where Secret Shadows Shine

Time Passes

In the dark
a body lies
alone
surrounded by cold
hard
uninvited truths
for winter company.
Outside the frosted pane
icicles hang like daggers
threatening to tear
through the fragile
veil of night.
If only
the slow
steady
tick
of the bedside clock
would quicken to the pace of racing thoughts.
But the morning sun cannot be hurried
to melt brutal weapons
suspended
in the dark.
This night must pass
as every night before,
no more swiftly
for the restless soul,
no more slowly
for the peaceful dreamer.
One night
the hands
will cease
to move,
and the ticking
will inevitably
stop.
Yet despite the broken timepiece
the day will break
and light return.

Alice Smith

Turn Around

In the misty mountain air
   heavy with autumn fog
   the fruit tree burdened with apples
   stands alone.
Down in the valley
   under the grayness of the same sky,
   the swimming hole
   filled with muddied water
   lies still.
Where is the little sapling
   that glistened with morning dew
   as the chirping child
   twiddled with the tiny twigs?
Where is the lake
   shimmering with afternoon reflections
   as the curly-headed girl
   squealed and splashed about?
The time has come to cut
   the heavy ringlets of regret
   and don a different point of view.
Turn around and wait
   for the morning sun
   to burn away the fog.
Pick a red delicious
   in the middle of the day
   and savor the sticky sweetness.
At the stroke of midnight
   swim naked in the moonlight
   and splash among the stars.

Talking to Truth

Tenacious, tactless truth,
How could you not conceive
I ached for vague veracity
To speed my mangled mending
And foster fairy tales
Of happy ever after endings?
Oh naked butcher of fantasy,
I pictured you in fuzzy gray
Where I would lay a weathered cheek
On a chamois shoulder of subtlety.

You are not what I expected,
No Prince of Peace or Charming.
But come inside and settle in.
Then show me what I need to know.

Shine your rays of realness
On the secrets stowed below.
Then play the chords of candor
Loud enough so I can hear,
But lower the lights and sweeten the sound
Before you hold me near.
Then dance me through the fragile steps
Of coming complications,
And rock me gently to the rhythmic beat
Of thumping, throbbing reality.

Alice Smith

Now That I Am Older

When I was younger I wanted to be older,
to shave my legs and wear high heels,
put Mama's lipstick on my mouth
and make a mess with make up.
To be a teen would be so cool
until I really was a teen,
and then I wished to be a bride,
all grown up and on my own.

Now that I am older, I'm wishing to feel younger.
The Revlon days of Fire and Ice fled by.
Today it's menthol Icy Hot
I spray on angry knees.
I loathe this pain preventing me from play,
but I love seeing my children who are grown
playing with children of their own.

The older I get the more I see
dismay and delight at every turn.
That pimple plague was coupled
with the promise of the prom,
and seasoned wisdom
comes with wrinkles and regret.
Balance is always present.
Nothing is ever perfect,
yet everything's complete.

Moving On

I travelled the well-worn path
to a crucial crossing.
That winding road
with each familiar turn
became a bumpy, gravel, wooded way
leading to a solitary dwelling place;
a tomb of unexplored loneliness.
I hibernated with troubling truths
for winter company
then awakened to the curious aroma
of something barely known.
I followed the foreign scent
creeping downward as I went
to empty out the iron skillet
smeared with something
old and stale.

I open every cabinet
looking for something fresh.
Sleeping senses revive
as I begin to cook
with flavorful ingredients
I have never used before.
Perhaps a mysterious meal awaits
if I relish this unfamiliarity.
I feel the melancholy of yesterday
beginning to slip away.
It's time to roll away the stone
and celebrate today.
I'll throw out all the no-fat fake
and slather butter on my bread.
I'll open a bottle of the finest wine
and drink a toast to moving on.

Alice Smith

When Pain Comes Knocking

When painful memories
come knocking
there are many ways to answer.
There are those who pretend
they never heard the knock
and some who slam the door
as soon as they get a glimpse
of what has come to call.
Others knock the knocker
down and hold the
injured party underfoot.
There are those who costume
the caller in clothing
more palatably pleasant
and even ones who relish the rapper,
holding on and never letting go.
A few invite the visitor
inside for conversation.
These lucky ones will
listen and learn
and know when the time
has come to kiss the caller
goodbye.

My Beautiful Sister

My beautiful sister.
I wept at the words
written on the back
of my picture
tucked away
in a drawer.
I usually dismissed her
as my cute little baby sister,
but she saw beauty in me
I wasn't able to see.
The number of years
between us remains the same,
but aging has sewn us
closer together.
Now I would never dismiss her,
my beautiful baby sister.

Alice Smith

My Best Friend

We were woven together
from the moment she was born.
We looked so much alike
people mistakenly thought
we were twins.
Other sisters fought
like cats and dogs,
but she and I
have always been
best friends.

Killing the Tooth Fairy

He tiptoed into my room and told me
the Tooth Fairy had forgotten him.
I'd been out late the night before,
was only half awake and unready
to pull the covers off. I lapsed into
a miserable moment of motherhood.
"My purse is on the floor over by the door."
I told him to take some dimes or a dollar,
whatever the fairy paid back then.
He looked at me, and shook his head.
"What do you mean?" was all he said.
Suddenly I was wide-awake.
"I'm sorry! I'm sorry! I thought you knew."
A hurried excuse for killing the innocent
dream of fairies flying through the night.
He mumbled,
"I thought...I kind of thought, but I didn't really *know*."
It only took a moment to replace a mysterious
fairy with a less than magical mom.
He picked up his money and wandered away.
I pulled up the covers and cried.

Alice Smith

Falling Apart

Two transparent spirits
Blown together
Floating in harmony
Formative beings intertwining
Clear and simple becoming opaque
Drifting apart
Splitting
Falling
Crash-landing
In separate heaps of earth
Hands digging alone
In the deep dark muddy ground
His fingers searching
Finding her familiar fingers
Caked with dirt
Tentative hands touching
Desperately clasping
Coming together
Letting go
Falling apart for good.

Binding Friendship

They held me together
when I was falling apart
and stuck with me
like glue
when I began to crack.
To them I'll adhere forever;
Jim and Barbara
and Jack!

My Only Brother

There were three of us
and only one of him.
He took a dive,
and the sisters
stayed afloat.
The girls huddled
with each other,
but when I hit rock bottom
I turned to my only brother.

Peace

Floating on the surface
paying no attention
to the bubbling below
in the deep
out of sight
held under
so it won't float up
splash me in the face
disturbing my peace.
Dare I dip my toe
in the water?
Make waves
in the smooth reflection?
What will happen
if I disturb the peace?

Alice Smith

Dream Mending

Grains of sand wear blisters on the sole.
A fragile face exposed to angry glare
Curses the cloudless sky.
Parched lips cry out
For the black umbrella of night,
But the penetrating light persists.

Raw redness plunges into salty emerald blue
Resisting the pull of undertow
Yet sinking deeper and deeper
Down through the weedy darkness
Into the fertile soil of sleep
Falling, falling, fading into the woods.

A naked figure roams through pungent pines
Hungrily hunting the laughing face and dancing pace
That hide beneath and between and behind.
Familiar places disappear then reappear
Overgrown with underbrush.
The woods seem empty, hushed, and still, yet

The hollow is stirring, pulsing, rumbling, waiting.
A tree frog croaks and crickets creak.
The dream is crazy alive.
White pines dancing,
Hoot owls laughing,
And moss is mending the sole.

Crawling into the Future

Drifting in the dark
forgetting
floating
in the harmless fluid of familiarity
protected in an embryonic curl
pushing through
the canal of pain
beautiful bloody flesh
emerging
smeared with nourishing juices
unfolding
waiting
to be wiped clean with a gentle touch.
The metamorphosis continues
in fertile surroundings of understanding.
A soft unprotected form
wiggling
squirming
peeking around
reaching out
crawling into the future.

Alice Smith

Brown

Divorce dumped me in the dirt.
I was trying to dig my way out
of the brown loneliness
when my best friend from way back when
tried to set me up and show me off
if only for a night.
Back in school she was a funny,
flighty, fashion queen,
making eyes at guys,
and overflowing with friendship ties.
I was the shy and quiet type,
but as I grew older I grew bolder
finding hidden hues in me
and taking them center-stage.
I felt grounded and deeply rooted,
blooming and living a colorful life.
But when I stepped into her home
I slouched into my teens
feeling that beige inferiority
peeking out from underground.
She showed me to my room
and told me how to dress.
I slipped into my long brown skirt
that hugged my hips
and showed off my shapely ankles.
The matching long-sleeve sweater
enhanced by a chunky amber necklace
created a comfortable combination.
I looked at my reflection
and smiled at the casual brown creation.
My confidence took a tumble
when I spied the shiny spikes
clacking down the stairs.
She clicked into the room
in a silky sleeveless mini-dress
showing lots of skin.
Her neck was wound in gobs of gold
and her wrists were bountifully bangled.
She looked like a lavender flibbertigibbet,
and I felt brown.

Moving Through the Walls

Memories pour from the old pine walls
Creating channels to bygone years
Of laughter and tears,
Wooded walks and dinner talks,
Christmas fires that glow and burn,
Curious boys who grow and learn
To make-believe,
To live and leave.

A moving whisper blows,
Whistling as it goes
Through the wall, telling all
To kiss the house and go.
Move away and know
The leaving time is right,
And love will live inside
These walls that hold the morning light.

Alice Smith

Breathing in the Dawn

A most unusual fear she had,
The girl with the curly hair.
She shuddered at the fluttering sound
Of wings upon a bird.
Not the slithering of the serpent
Or the spider's creepy crawl,
But feathers flapping frightened her
For reasons unbeknown.
Silent nocturnal soaring dreams
Took her up to the top of the world,
But she had no pair of feather wings
For they would make a noise.
One night while she was sleeping
Wings were painted on her back,
Each feather formed with careful stroke
By a hand she knew so well,
The habit of the fingers
Giving pleasure as they moved
Up and down behind her
With a soothing tickle touch.
When the girl awakened
She was perched upon the sill
Breathing in the dawn
Outside the darkened room.
She felt the feathers on her back
And made a flutter sound.
She saw the painter's beckoning hand
then leapt into the light.

Winter Light

A gray and ponderous sky
sheds minimal light on winter limbs.
Twisted, misshapen, exposed;
a haunting skeleton displayed.
Dusk dissolves to black
peppered with points of light.
Yesterday's bony branches
wear early-morning frost coats
as dawn gives birth to blue
streaked with pastel whimsy.
The diamond twigs shiver and creak
until the source of light
melts away the winter garments
worn for sheer protection.
A sudden breath of warmer wind
fired by noon-day brilliance
whispers to the naked boughs
a promise billowing with blossom.
The leafless limbs inhale the hope
of emerald resurrection
as sunset colors wash the sky
in vivid confirmation.

Alice Smith

Liz

She put herself
together differently,
mixing unlikely
combinations with unique
artistic style.
Her passing
created a hole
filled with
forget me nots.

Donna Juan and I

Donna Juan emerged one day
   from somewhere in the deep.
She threw me into cyberspace
   finding fellows to replace
   the hollow hole within.
We tore into a fairy tale
   looking for a Camelot.
Finding it was not
   a Sleepless in Seattle ending
   but perhaps a chapter-one
   of stories just beginning.
Oh it was a dizzy dance
   drawing in a dozen dudes
   to mambo through the motions,
   to sip the cyber-potions,
   to cycle all around
   discovering hidden ground.
She imbued me with a strut
   and showed me how to soar
   to now-familiar places
   that before were foreign spaces.
Ah those spaces filled with places
   made the journey worth the while.
The frantic search for someone died
   when someone wanted me.
There was ending and beginning.
That's when Donna closed her eyes.
She was fading.
She was fading.
So I stepped into her feet
   and felt her wings repeat.
Then we flew to inner space
   and kissed the past goodbye.
We've settled in together,
   old Donna Juan and I.

Alice Smith

Living On

The first time around
they couldn't see each other
for it was bad luck.
She was upstairs dressing.
He was downstairs waiting.
The organ hidden in the family den
was played by a rented stranger.
Joyful music had been requested,
but a funereal sound filled the air
as her father walked her down
and handed her away.
The boy in black and the girl in white
recited solemn vows
and thumb-wrestled in secret
while they were holding hands.
No one can remember now
which thumb won,
but twenty-eight years later
the marriage lost.

The second time around they dressed together
in the house that would become their home.
Her dress was the color of his pale-blue eyes.
His suit a version of the grayer blue of hers.
This time her father was seated with her mother
as the couple walked together down the aisle
to the joyful sound of a friend's guitar.
The man and woman looked into each other's eyes
and repeated sacred vows without the word obey.
At ceremony's end Isaiah's blessing was read:
"You will go out in joy and be led forth in peace;
the mountains and hills will burst forth in song before you,
and all the trees of the field will clap their hands."
Spontaneously, friends and family broke into applause,
while arm in arm the couple left to strumming alleluias,
and the marriage is living on.

Seeing the Ordinary

A published poem was sent to me
by a friend who sends me poetry.
I had never published
a single word or phrase,
but still I wondered why
this poet chose
such common things to praise.

A chalk mark on the sidewalk,
a yellow-jacket's nest,
a tea stain on the counter,
a khaki fishing vest,
a baby in a stroller,
a rabbit in the rain.
I haven't stolen words from him.
I'm simply showing
how commonplace his choices were
in what he saw and wrote.

Then it finally hit me,
and I opened up to see
the extraordinary beauty
in his ordinary day.
Now the wonder of his words
is sinking in somehow
for he opened me
to feel a fascination
with the now.

Alice Smith

Where Would You Rather Be?

Tranquil travelers
savoring their surroundings
trickle down the tree-lined trails
populated with wondrous matter
as agitated drivers pour
into a black sea of asphalt.

The soft percussion
of the silver mountain falls
draws curious companions
down through a wooded maze
while competitive consumers try to beat each other
to that precious piece of pavement closest to the store.

A young man sits silently listening
to the familiar tune of a bobwhite
and absentmindedly
whistles an imitation
while voracious shoppers scream
for more unnecessary matter.

Under the protective branches
of a spreading maple
a father will succumb to his child's familiar plea
to stay a little longer, to tell another tale,
but an acquisitive mother in a hurried hustle
dismisses the disturbance of her toddler's restless whimpers.

The magical spectacle
of twilight's multi-colored splendor
draws evening couples to the open western brow
to partake of nature's nightly offering
while the mall rats march to their vehicles
securely locked in the blacktop desert.

My Father

My father was the king
of sarcasm and seduction,
wrapped in a robe that sucked you in
and turned you inside out.

Sarcasm and seduction
put you off and pulled you in
and turned you inside out.
Both mighty king and ordinary man

Put you off and pulled you in
Unexpected rage and unconditional love
made the mighty king an ordinary man
many feared and many praised.

Unexpected rage and unconditional love
were wrapped in a robe that sucked you in.
Many feared and many praised
my father who was king.

Alice Smith

The Upper Lake

I walk along the wooded path
    that leads to a sacred spot
    flooded with the past,
    drenched in the present,
    and spilling over into the future.
The surface ripples with reflections
    reminding me that what I see
    mixes memory with reality.
The lake lined with evergreens
    is dotted with demise
    of ancient hemlocks older than I.
Death makes me want to cry
    when I see the naked limbs
    stranded in the sky.
But when I bow my head
    and see the barren branches
    mirrored in the water,
    the blight is blurred
    and death is beautifully blended in.
I don't know what I was looking for
    when I came to the lake today,
    yet I always find something
    floating up and sinking in.
This family piece of peace
    is one of those thin places
    that feels like multiple spaces
    spliced together with mystery
    and pointing to eternity.

Reflections

I see a picture of him
standing on the bridge
reflected in the water
where his ashes
were sprinkled at dawn.
His nature inhabits
every corner of this place
where I feel him
living on.

Alice Smith

Two Lovers

They bring me life,
my unconditional lovers!
The moment I open the door
a little ball of instincts bounces by my side
and smells what I have seen.
The upright understanding one
takes me where I am and asks me how I've been.
I fondle the fluff and melt into the hunk,
feeling the furry fun of loving a marvelous male.

I laugh at the logic
that lives between two legs
and sees my sags and stretches
as a form of ageless beauty.
When I look in the mirror
a wrinkled spotted moon stares back at me,
but he sees a winter sunset
reflected in the sea.

On cold and cranky days
I hear my bark and wince.
The fuzzy friend with paws
is deaf to my off-key tone,
cuddling close, warming my toes,
doing what he knows.
My voice to him is music,
and my smelly socks perfume.

Oh if I could see myself
the way my lovers do,
I'd shed my shabby shawl
of camouflaged protection
and lap up all about me
from a different point of view.

A Place Where Secret Shadows Shine

Simply Being There

When my father died
the Lhasa howled,
the children cried,
but Mom put off her grieving.
After the funeral
we sucked our mother into smoking;
not something we often do.
We hoped to help her blow away the pain,
but the mourning party was too much for her
so she took her little dog to bed and cuddled
what she'd shared with Dad.

Years later she was sitting on her porch
wearing sunny-morning yellow,
holding that little Lhasa on her lap.
Tears were messing up my face
as I watched my mother carry
her little love and climb into my car.
I never knew how long a drive half a mile could be.
The vet was kind.
The death was peaceful,
but not for Mom and me.
We sobbed and hugged;
not something we often do.
We took the same route home, but it was even longer.
She said she'd lost her link to Dad.
I nodded, but I wondered,
What was I?
Over and over she thanked me
for simply being there.

That morning death was the overture
to a motherless symphony.
Off and on all day I cried and tried
to drown out the deadly drum.
She was home alone, sitting in sunset yellow
when I walked onto her porch
and she sucked me into smoking.
Together we inhaled the morning sadness,
and I tried to blow away the pain.

Alice Smith

One day I won't be able to thank her
for simply being there.

Curly Hair

When I was a little girl I hated my curly hair.
I wanted it long and straight,
but Mama kept it short,
and Daddy tried to fix the frizz
with Brylcreem made for men.
When I was all grown up with children of my own
I'd figured out a way to flatten out the frizz.
One day while picking up my son from school
I thought my hair looked smooth and cool.
He hit me with a question that sadly set me straight.
"Mom, have you ever had
that long and flowing sort of hair,
or has it always been the bush-up kind?"
I looked in the rearview mirror
and saw just what he saw
then sadly had to answer,
"It was never long and flowing."

What he had I'd always wanted,
shiny, blonde, and straight,
but then he gave me something better
than any hair could be.
My questioning boy
grew into a man and gave me
a bald-headed bundle of joy.
The night that she was born
I held her in my arms sitting by her dad
listening to Alison Krauss
singing the song *I Will...*
love you forever and forever,
and I know I will.
After a couple of years she showed a couple of curls.
The one who captured my heart also captured my hair,
but she loves her curls and tells the girls
she got her hair from Ami.
If she loves that part of her that came from a part of me
I'll put away the iron and embrace what I came by naturally.
Ah me!

Alice Smith

Dreams Can Change

I lived the life of a little girl
growing up on Lookout,
the mountain in the famous speech
of Martin Luther King.
There were no colored children
in my school or in my pool.
They learned and played
in a separate but "equal" space.
Their mothers lived on the place.
We drank from different fountains
and dined in different diners.
I didn't know to dare to dream
of righting this wretched wrong.
Motherhood was the only dream
I managed to materialize,
but others marched and multiplied
seeing the pain in long division.

My grandchild got a different start
at Battle Elementary,
a far more colorful place
where children played together
and learned a different race.
One day that little girl
took me by the hand and led me
to the changing room
where her dancing clothes were stored.
She took off everything
and twirled around in nothing.
Her dance was interrupted
when a speedy little boy
crashed into the common room
and stripped to use the potty.
I stood there smiling
at unselfconscious blended beauty.
No one blinked and no one stared
at the naked difference in color and in gender.

Wedding Picture

The Family Farm nestled in the redwoods
was a fairytale setting for a summer wedding.
I was pretty in pink sitting beside my spouse.
A little farther down the pew
sat my former husband with his wife in navy blue.

I watched my son as he waited for his bride
to join him under the trees and recite creative vows.
He swore to feed her sweets forever.
She pledged to be his playmate.
When the married couple kissed, the clapping couldn't wait.

We gathered in the woods for pictures.
First the family of the bride,
Then the family of the groom,
which was later divided in two.
We were forming groups as we were told to do.

The groom requested a picture
with his father and his mother.
The camera recreated something from the past.
Our son was in between; blending together the three.
When we parted he said, "Thanks for making me."

Alice Smith

Somewhere Over the Rainbow

They were somewhere over there,
and I was so far over here.
He texted me to pray
for his wife and child to be.
What my son was asking
was terrifying me.
He finally called to tell me
he had a healthy little girl,
but his wife was still in danger
and he was in a crumbling world.
I wanted to hug my baby boy
and hold his baby girl,
but they were somewhere over there,
and I was so far over here.
The messages were mixed
as to what was going on.
I tried to hold myself together
when someone played
my favorite song.
Perhaps I'll wish upon a star
and wake up where the clouds
are far behind me.
I burst into pent-up tears of joy
when my phone produced a picture
of a land in a lullaby.
His wife had finally wakened
and held their baby in her arms.
If happy little bluebirds fly
beyond the rainbow
why oh why can't I?
So I hopped a plane
and flew to somewhere over there
to hug my baby boy
and hold his baby girl.
Everyone would soon be fine,
and way up high the skies were blue.
The dreams that I dared to dream
really did come true.

Bumping and Twirling

He wiped a bugger
on the dash
of his grandfather's brand-new car.
That's just what little boys do.
I should know.
I had two.
Burps and farts
got laughs and applause
taking center-stage
while verbal communication
sat in the nosebleed section
as I played the mother
directing a masculine play.
I see my grandson
like his father and his uncle,
banging like a boy,
bumping right along,
always out there doing something,
cutting to the chase.
My own little boys have turned into men,
and both have given me
one of the other kind
allowing me a grownup view
of one from my own gender.
They twirl around in tutus
and play around with hairdos
bundles of emoting chatter
always in there feeling something
that may or may not matter.
I grew up as one of them many years ago,
but then I was only being,
and now I'm really seeing
the different way we feminine creatures grow.

Alice Smith

Her in Me

A friendship seed was planted
lingering over lunch
as tangy tales were told
with hers resembling mine.
The natural sweetness in her voice
tasted faintly familiar.
Listening to this woman
and hearing wholeness ring,
I wondered if she could hear
harmony from me.
I focused on our likeness,
which was comforting yet eerie.
I saw so much of her in me
I felt like I was she.

After the meal we parted ways,
but our paths continued crossing.
I see her clearer than before.
She's sprinkled with unique
gems of generosity and sterling hospitality.
The door is always open to her culinary kindness,
and her den of warmth is a peaceful place to rest.
Once I recognized her worth
I couldn't help myself.
I started wishing I could see
much more of her in me.

When I saw her deeply rooted
and me as simply shallow,
dusk dimmed into darkness
and shined on my projection.
In blackest night mysterious light
hides behind a dreaming door.
This deeply rooted wonder
opened me to see
that when I find her in my dreams
she is a part of me.

Nelson's Pitcher

At first glance
a white pottery pitcher
encircled with scripted black
didn't strike me as artistic
and made me wonder why
the giver saw such meaning
in this plain and primitive piece.
The giver of the gift
saw my double-sided view of life
pouring from the pitcher when she read
the famous words of Dickens
circling 'round the vessel.
It was the best of times.
It was the worst of times.
And on and on it goes.
There is no clear duality.
Only mysterious reality.
The artist chose black and white
to convey the well-known words
that mix the shades of best and worst,
and seasons of darkness and light.
There's beautiful wisdom if one can believe
the incredulous power of foolishness.
The scripted space runs out at the base.
It's the spring of hope. It's the winter of...
No room for despair on a pitcher given in love.

Alice Smith

Evolving

There was no original perfection.
It was a long and complicated evolution
  from matter
    to life
      to consciousness
      to self-consciousness.*
I haven't fallen from anywhere.
I'm planted in the ground of being.
  Evolving
    Searching
      Dreaming
        Holding on
        to Almighty affirmation
        that accepts me as I am
        and empowers me to be

*Bishop John Shelby Spong gave me permission to quote his words.

Dream Work

While drifting in the dark of night
I feel an opening in the space
by bending away the rods of rote
and letting the wandering words take wing,
magically compounding the common clutter
in artistic arrangement of things unknown.

Crawl into the vestibule to vastness
and absorb the world of dreams,
a mysterious deposit from the deep Divine
bubbling up and breaking in,
a place where secret shadows shine
and undiscovered understanding thrives.

In the bright of day what's mine is mine,
but the dark of dream frays the seam
sewing the seeds where nightmares bloom
into glorious gifts from the giver within.
Unwrap these presents in time with care
and waken to a wider way.

Alice Smith

Knotted Nots

Being tied
to ancient creeds
and literal interpretation
created a knot in me.
Untangling myself
from what became
my nots
set me free
to see
the mystery
that laces
us together.

Something Missing

Once they crossed from east to west
she felt lost.
She didn't know this place
a block or two removed
from being Mrs. Someone.
Her missing husband's Upper East Side pattern
was lavish and familiar.
This wafting whiff of regularity
smelled of something less
and something more.
That first night
before she dimmed the hotel lights
she noticed something missing.
Her wallet and a pack of prunes;
a very curious pair.
One kept her identity,
The other her regularity.
Too tired to dawdle in the dark,
the search would have to wait.
When daylight broke
she looked in every pocket,
tore through every drawer,
shook the sheets and swept the suite
but came up empty-handed.
Everyone in the party searched,
but no one found what she had lost.
A theft was what it had to be,
but the missing pack of prunes?
That was the mystery.
They canceled cards and licenses
and called security
laughingly suspecting a constipated thief.
When the West Side weekend ended
she was grateful she had lived a little
but knew she'd lost a lot.
Unpacking baggage
in the safety of her home
she saw the wallet and the prunes
where they had always been.
Her regular identity,

Alice Smith

she had it once again!
She plopped the prunes aside
and tucked her wallet in her purse.
She thought she had it all,
but something still was missing.

Acceptance

Happiness flows
from true acceptance,
no matter what I'm given.
If I am consumed
with how life ought to be,
unhappiness swallows me.

Alice Smith

Making a Mark

A father makes a mark.
It matters not if he is real
or grand or step
or never even met.
An impression
of neglect
lets imagination
run rampant
for better or for worse.
He could be
a burning brand
of subtle abuse
bruising and battering
the fragile worth
of the innocent child,
or a trace of tenderness
drawn with care
and rendered with affection
erasing the separating lines
and creating an intersection.
The farsighted father figure
leaves unconditional love notes
written in permanent ink
and sealed with a stamp of approval.

Something New

I think I'm looking for something new,
    he said.
At least he didn't say someone,
    which I had heard before.
I asked,
    For what?
I don't know,
    he said.
I'm waiting for something.
You can't just sit there waiting,
    I said.
Waiting for something like what?
    I pushed.
I'm waiting to be grabbed,
    he said,
By what?
    I prodded.
He shrugged but didn't answer.
Grabbed by the unknown?
    I asked.
He shrugged.
He smiled.
He nodded yes.

Alice Smith

Buried Anger Takes Flight

I try to bury myself in an airport book,
but from time to time I take a look
at what is going on around me.
Look at that slutty tattooed tart
with shapely legs like mine
traveling in heels so high she trips
and tumbles, tearing to make her flight.
And that silver-headed prick makes me sick.
He's old enough to be my father
shuffling down the concourse
with a bosom babe, half his age.
You look ridiculous, you parading piece of shit!
Damn, my flight has been delayed.
I sigh and glare at the woman
waiting next to me with withered
hands that match my own.
The bitch believes she's beautiful,
clothed in Coco Chanel,
but her fucking face is stretched
and pulled into something
resembling a burn from hell.
My iPhone strum distracts me,
but it's his instead of mine.
I can't escape the cocky dick's
self-important yelling,
making demands of a person I pity
though we've never even met.
Holy crap, there's been another delay.
I want to bawl like the bitchin' baby
shrieking across the way.
Ok, she's restless just like me,
but I hope to God she isn't seated in 4A.
I'm starving, but when I spy the enormous man
stuffing pizza in his mouth
standing by the garbage can
it makes me want to puke.
Come on, give me a break!
Don't let this monster be my
seatmate filling up his space
and spilling over into half of mine.

A Place Where Secret Shadows Shine

Yikes, trapped between the bawling and the blubber!
Is there a normal person in this place?
I wonder what these airport assholes see
when they take a look at me
buried in my Danielle Steel
romantic fantasy.

Wow, I Carried On!

I usually check my anger,
but today I actually
carried on
and pulled it
along with me.
I'd rather let
the baggage handler
do the heavy lifting,
but packed inside
my personal tote
were things with which
I rarely travel,
and I didn't want to take
the risk of losing
what I need.
I stored it
in the overhead
then pulled it down
and rolled it out with me.

Out of our Control

Why do we think we can save the daylight?
Every year we spring forward
into the hope of the coming season,
savoring the extra hour of light
at the end of every day.
When autumn takes its turn
we fall back under the cover
that morning darkness will disappear
an hour sooner than yesterday.
The only control we have
is changing the hands
on the clocks.
We cannot reduce the dark
or lengthen the light
for time is out of our hands.

Alice Smith

Kenyan Kindness

I climbed the stairs
and opened the door
to the home of people
I had never met before.
They burst into song.
I burst into tears.
Strangers singing
words I didn't understand
in a language I didn't know
took me in and fed me food
filled with foreign flavors.
Unfamiliarity tends to make
me want to turn into a turnip
buried underground.
My paleness and my plainness
in the midst of their black beauty
began to brighten
as the women swirled around
me in their sacred scarves and skirts.
Splendid singing souls
in brightly colored clothes
were blending black and white.
Simple surroundings soaked in
Kenyan kindness brought to life
a foreign part of me
I had never met before.

Filling the Home

I imagined my sister's interior overflowing with ornamentation as she described her Dallas decorations. Her elaborate joy over holiday embellishment left me feeling unadorned. It was time to decorate but I wasn't in the mood. What my sister did so lovingly, I did grudgingly; stomping as I went from the basement back to the den, over and over again. I wasn't feeling Christmas in my heart, only in my knees. The arthritic attempt at creating a festive feel left me in a sinking spell. Then I remembered a humorous gift I had received the year before. I found my present in the kitchen drawer and pulled it out for decoration. Displaying the comic truth* brightened my home with a spot of Christmas cheer.

*"She was one plum pudding away from a yuletide meltdown." (on a cocktail napkin)

Dreaming Differently

In 1959 we never dreamed
we could be something other
than the women we saw
portrayed on our TV.
They wore aprons tying them to home,
staying in the background
while men were free to rise and roam.

In 1999 I had a dream come true
in the form of a baby girl;
a grandchild who would live and grow
in a far more open world
dreaming differently
than I had ever dared.

One Christmas she drew for me
a picture of a person
with black and curly hair.
She proudly described this person
as our future president.
Since the face was rather brown I asked,
"Is that Barack Obama?"
"No," said the little eight-year-old.
"That's a picture of ME!"

A Place Where Secret Shadows Shine

Living in the Loop

I was traveling around
a loop in the woods.
The path was clearly tended.
I easily avoided
the stray twig or tiny branch
that had fallen from above.
The sky was sapphire blue,
and the breeze smelled
of savory September.
Pine needles and colored leaves
softened the ground
beneath my feet.
Nature was nurturing me,
surrounding me with her peaceful beauty.
Then suddenly
my hike was hindered,
and my way was blocked.
I sat stuck on the trunk of a fallen oak
and cursed its uninvited presence.
That which had given me
this awesome autumn afternoon
now had thrown this monster in my path.
My tendency was to turn around
and retrace the ground
that had brought me to this barrier.
But I longed to see the other side
of what was in my way.
So I climbed and clawed
and made it through the tangled mess.
It was worth the scrapes and bruises
for the last part of the loop
was the loveliest of all.

Alice Smith

Saving Thyme

A long time ago
the grass included so much thyme
the children's dirty clothes
were herb-scented
after rolling down the hills
for hours at a time.
Someone got the notion
to purify the lawn.
No wandering weeds or fragrant herbs
would mingle with the grass.
It wasn't going to be the way it used to be.
But that thyme had meaning to me!
When I squished a couple of sprigs
between my fingers
I could smell the children's clothes
or taste the corn and tomato salad
the herb would later flavor.
During the herbal eradication
I found a living patch of thyme
mixed into the moss meandering
onto a small stone bridge
and begged that it be left alone.
There's not as much as
there used to be,
but every summer I go to the bridge
to check on the thyme I saved.

Time after Time

Time after time
they washed the dinner dishes,
wiped the kitchen counter
and corked the Cabernet.
The soothing supper music was
mixed with clanging pots and pans
being put away.
It was a night like any other,
or so she thought.
Then he took her in his arms,
and the kitchen noises ceased
as the music drew them in.
She placed her wrinkled cheek
on his soft cotton shoulder
as they swirled between
the sink and stove
and waltzed around the oven.
Her needy knees were nimble.
His hurting hip was healed.
They were really cookin',
and the aches and pains took wing
as two old married lovers swayed to
Time after Time.

Alice Smith

Such a Kind

I am sitting in the dark
viewing the projection.
Unexpected words
from a poignant
romantic-comedy
unravel me.
Find a person who is kind.
Such a quest
had never crossed my mind.
I blink the blurring liquid
from my eyes
and swallow the lump
settling in my throat
for here I am
sitting next to such a kind.

My Lonely Shoes

The shoes I used to wear
are sitting in the closet
wishing to be worn,
wanting to be needed,
but they're not.

They've forgotten
what it feels like
to cushion my soles
and support my ankles
as I move about

lunging for a lob,
running for a short shot,
or waiting out the opposition
being a patient
human backboard.

They sit there
on the upper shelf
waiting for me
to pull them down
and put them back in play.

Perhaps this year
my lonely tennis
shoes and I
will find a way
to somehow reunite.

Alice Smith

Floating in the Balance

Stretched between
black locust tree
and white pine
a criss cross
hammock
holds me
in the grayness.
The hook
screwed into the locust
pulls out,
and I fall
from the mysterious middle.
I must bore another hole
into the blackness
to hook the hammock
that holds me
floating in the balance.

What Is

If you can
tell me where
I'm going
after I leave here,
I won't be
going there.
The other side
of life is
mystery.
It's not an up
or down there.
I'm going somewhere
that cannot be described
in terms of time and space
and who will be there
and who will not.
I'm going to what is...
and so are you.

Alice Smith

The Garden and the Lake

Where do you want your ashes scattered?
First the garden in the churchyard,
following the routine ritual.
The priest can pray the written words
heard every time
remains of strangers,
friends, and relatives
are planted in the ground.
Mix me in the soil of souls
as part of something holy and mysterious.
But save a piece of me,
and travel to the Upper Lake
where sacred mystery lives,
and written prayers are never needed.
Fill your glass with spirits
and toast the life that lives among us.
Bless the bountiful beauty.
Then let me go in the holy water.